THREE PLAYS

OHIO IMPROMPTU
CATASTROPHE
WHAT WHERE

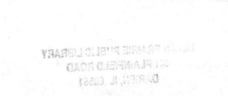

Works by Samuel Beckett Published by Grove Press

Cascando and Other Short Dramatic Pieces (Words and Music;
    Eh Joe; Play; Come and Go; Film [original version])
Collected Poems in English & French
The Collected Shorter Plays of Samuel Beckett
The Collected Works of Samuel Beckett [twenty-five volumes]
Company
Disjecta
Endgame
Ends and Odds (Not I; That Time; Footfalls; Ghost Trio; . . . but the
    clouds . . . ; Theatre I; Theatre II; Radio I; Radio II)
Film, A Film Script
First Love and Other Shorts (From an Abandoned Work; Enough,
    Imagination Dead Imagine; Ping; Not I; Breath)
Fizzles
Happy Days
How It Is
I Can't Go On, I'll Go On: A Selection from Samuel Beckett's Work
Ill Seen Ill Said
Krapp's Last Tape and Other Dramatic Pieces (All That Fall; Embers
    [a play for radio]; Act Without Words I and II [mimes])
The Lost Ones
Malone Dies
Mercier and Camier
Molloy
More Pricks Than Kicks
Murphy
Poems in English
Proust
Ohio Impromptu, Catastrophe, and What Where: Three Plays
Rockaby and Other Short Pieces (Ohio Impromptu; All Strange
    Away; A Piece of Monologue)
Stories and Texts for Nothing
Three Novels (Molloy; Malone Dies; The Unnamable)
Waiting for Godot
Watt
Worstward Ho

THREE PLAYS

OHIO IMPROMPTU
CATASTROPHE
WHAT WHERE

by Samuel Beckett

This material was purchased as part of an
Indian Prairie Public Library District grant
**"Our Multicultural Neighborhood:
Promoting Awareness."**
Funding for this grant was provided by the
Illinois State Library, a division of the Office of the
Secretary of State, using federal LSTA funding

GROVE PRESS
New York

The name Grove Press and the colophon printed on the outside
of this book are trademarks registered in the U.S. Patent and
Trademark Office and in other countries.

Published by Grove Press
a division of Wheatland Corporation
841 Broadway
New York, N.Y. 10003

ISBN: 0-8021-5116-7
Library of Congress Catalog Card Number: 83-49372

Printed in the United States of America

This book is printed on acid-free paper.

First Grove Press Edition 1984
First Evergreen Edition 1984
5   4   3   2

Ohio Impromptu

Ohio Impromptu was first performed in the Drake Union, Stadium 2 Theatre, in association with Ohio State University, on May 9, 1981. It was directed by Alan Schneider.

Reader	David Warrilow
Listener	Rand Mitchell

●

Ohio Impromptu was produced by Lucille Lortel and The Harold Clurman Theatre, New York, New York, on June 15, 1983. It was directed by Alan Schneider.

Reader	David Warrilow
Listener	Rand Mitchell

L = *Listener.*
R = *Reader.*
As alike in appearance as possible.

*Light on table midstage. Rest of stage in darkness.
Plain white deal table, say 8' x 4'. Two plain
armless white deal chairs.*

L *seated at table facing front towards end of
long side audience right. Bowed head propped
on right hand. Face hidden. Left hand on table.
Long black coat. Long white hair.*

R *seated at table in profile centre of short side
audience right. Bowed head propped on right
hand. Left hand on table. Book on table before
him open at last pages. Long black coat. Long
white hair.*

Black wide-brimmed hat at centre of table.

Fade up.

Ten seconds.

R *turns page.*
Pause.

R *(reading)*: Little is left to tell. In a last—

L *knocks with left hand on table.*

Little is left to tell.

Pause. Knock.

In a last attempt to obtain relief he moved from
where they had been so long together to a
single room on the far bank. From its single
window he could see the downstream extremity
of the Isle of Swans.

Pause.

Relief he had hoped would flow from
unfamiliarity. Unfamiliar room. Unfamiliar

scene. Out to where nothing ever shared. Back
to where nothing ever shared. From this he had
once half hoped some measure of relief might
flow.

Pause.

Day after day he could be seen slowly pacing
the islet. Hour after hour. In his long black coat
no matter what the weather and old world
Latin Quarter hat. At the tip he would always
pause to dwell on the receding stream. How in
joyous eddies its two arms conflowed and flowed
united on. Then turn and his slow steps retrace.

Pause.

In his dreams—

Knock.

Then turn and his slow steps retrace.

Pause. Knock.

● 13

In his dreams he had been warned against this change. Seen the dear face and heard the unspoken words, Stay where we were so long alone together, my shade will comfort you.

Pause.

Could he not—

Knock.

Seen the dear face and heard the unspoken words, Stay where we were so long alone together, my shade will comfort you.

Pause. Knock.

Could he not now turn back? Acknowledge his error and return to where they were once so long alone together. Alone together so much shared. No. What he had done alone could not be undone. Nothing he had ever done alone could ever be undone. By him alone.

Pause.

In this extremity his old terror of night laid hold on him again. After so long a lapse that as if never been. *(Pause. Looks closer.)* Yes, after so long a lapse that as if never been. Now with redoubled force the fearful symptoms described at length page forty paragraph four. *(Starts to turn back the pages. Checked by L's left hand. Resumes relinquished page.)* White nights now again his portion. As when his heart was young. No sleep no braving sleep till—*(turns page)* —dawn of day.

Pause.

Little is left to tell. One night

Knock.

Little is left to tell.

Pause. Knock.

One night as he sat trembling head in hands
from head to foot a man appeared to him and
said, I have been sent by—and here he named
the dear name—to comfort you. Then drawing
a worn volume from the pocket of his long
black coat he sat and read till dawn. Then
disappeared without a word.

Pause.

Some time later he appeared again at the same
hour with the same volume and this time without
preamble sat and read it through again the long
night through. Then disappeared without a
word

Pause.

So from time to time unheralded he would
appear to read the sad tale through again and
the long night away. Then disappear without a
word.

Pause.

With never a word exchanged they grew to be
as one.

Pause.

Till the night came at last when having closed
the book and dawn at hand he did not disappear
but sat on without a word.

Pause.

Finally he said, I have had word from— and
here he named the dear name—that I shall not
come again. I saw the dear face and heard the
unspoken words, No need to go to him again,
even were it in your power.

Pause.

So the sad—

Knock.

Saw the dear face and heard the unspoken
words, No need to go to him again, even were
it in your power.

Pause. Knock.

So the sad tale a last time told they sat on as
though turned to stone. Through the single
window dawn shed no light. From the street no
sound of reawakening. Or was it that buried in
who knows what thoughts they paid no heed?
To light of day. To sound of reawakening. What
thoughts who knows. Thoughts, no, not
thoughts. Profounds of mind. Buried in who
knows what profounds of mind. Of mindlessness.
Whither no light can reach. No sound. So sat
on as though turned to stone. The sad tale a
last time told.

Pause.

Nothing is left to tell.

Pause. **R** *makes to close book.*

Knock. Book half-closed.

Nothing is left to tell.

Pause. **R** *closes book.*

Knock.

Silence. Five seconds.

Simultaneously they lower their right hands to table, raise their heads and look at each other. Unblinking. Expressionless.

Ten seconds.

Fade out.

Catastrophe

FOR VACLAV HAVEL

Catastrophe was first performed at The Avignon Festival, Avignon, France, on July 21, 1982. It was directed by Stephan Meldegg.

The Protagonist	Pierre Arditi
The Director	Gerard Desarthe
The Assistant	Stephanie Loik

•

Catastrophe was first produced in the United States by Lucille Lortel and The Harold Clurman Theatre, New York, New York, on June 15, 1983. It was directed by Alan Schneider.

Protagonist	David Warrilow
The Director	Donald Davis
His Assistant	Margaret Reed
Luke	Bond Mitchell

Director (D).

His female assistant (A).

Protagonist (P).

Luke, *in charge of the lighting, offstage* **(L).**

Rehearsal. Final touches to the last scene. Bare stage. **A** *and* **L** *have just set the lighting.* **D** *has just arrived.*

D *in an armchair downstage audience left. Fur coat. Fur toque to match. Age and physique unimportant.*

A *standing beside him. White overall. Bare head. Pencil on ear. Age and physique unimportant.*

P *midstage standing on a black block 18 inches high. Black wide-brimmed hat. Black dressing-gown to ankles. Barefoot. Head bowed. Hands in pockets. Age and physique unimportant.*

D *and* **A** *contemplate* **P***. Long pause.*

A: *(Finally).* Like the look of him?

D: So so. *(Pause.)* Why the plinth?

A: To let the stalls see the feet.

Pause.

D: Why the hat?

A: To help hide the face.

Pause.

D: Why the gown?

A: To have him all black.

Pause.

D: What has he on underneath? *(A moves towards P.)* Say it.

A *halts.*

A: His night attire.

D: Colour?

A: Ash.

D *takes out a cigar.*

D: Light. (**A** *returns, lights the cigar, stands still.* **D** *smokes.)* How's the skull?

A: You've seen it.

D: I forget. (**A** *moves towards* **P**.) Say it.

A *halts.*

A: Moulting. A few tufts.

D: Colour?

A: Ash.

Pause.

D: Why hands in pockets?

A: To help have him all black.

D: They mustn't.

A: I make a note. *(She takes out a pad, takes pencil, notes.)* Hands exposed.
She puts back pad and pencil.

D: How are they? (**A** *at a loss. Irritably.*) The hands, how are the hands?

A: You've seen them.

D: I forget.

A: Crippled. Fibrous degeneration.

D: Clawlike?

A: If you like.

D: Two claws?

A: Unless he clench his fists.

D: He mustn't.

A: I make a note. *(She takes out pad, takes pencil, notes.)* Hands limp.

She puts back pad and pencil.

D: Light. *(A returns, relights the cigar, stands still. D smokes.)* Good. Now let's have a look. *(A at a loss. Irritably.)* Get going. Lose that gown. *(He consults his chronometer.)* Step on it, I have a caucus.

A goes to P, takes off the gown. P submits, inert. A steps back, the gown over her arm. P in old grey pyjamas, head bowed, fists clenched. Pause.

A: Like him better without? *(Pause.)* He's shivering.

D: Not all that. Hat.

A *advances, takes off hat, steps back, hat in hand. Pause.*

A: Like that cranium?

D: Needs whitening.

A: I make a note. *(She takes out pad, takes pencil, notes.)* Whiten cranium.

She puts back pad and pencil.

D: The hands. *(A at a loss. Irritably.)* The fists. Get going. *(A advances, unclenches fists, steps back.)* And whiten.

A: I make a note. *(She takes out pad, takes pencil, notes.)* Whiten hands.

She puts back pad and pencil. They contemplate
P.

D: *(Finally)*. Something wrong. *(Distraught.)*
What is it?

A: *(Timidly)*. What if we were to . . . were
to . . . join them?

D: No harm trying. *(A advances, joins the
hands, steps back.)* Higher. *(A advances, raises
waist-high the joined hands, steps back.)* A
touch more. *(A advances, raises breast-high the
joined hands.)* Stop! *(A steps back.)* Better. It's
coming. Light.

A returns, relights cigar, stands still. D smokes.

A: He's shivering.

D: Bless his heart. *Pause.*

A: *(Timidly)*. What about a little . . . a little . . .
gag?

D: For God's sake! This craze for explication! Every i dotted to death! Little gag! For God's sake!

A: Sure he won't utter?

D: Not a squeak. *(He consults his chronometer.)* Just time. I'll go and see how it looks from the house.

*Exit **D**, not to appear again. **A** subsides in the armchair, springs to her feet no sooner seated, takes out a rag, wipes vigorously back and seat of chair, discards rag, sits again. Pause.*

D: *(Off, plaintive).* I can't see the toes. *(Irritably).* I'm sitting in the front row of the stalls and can't see the toes.

A: *(Rising).* I make a note. *(She takes out pad, takes pencil, notes.)* Raise pedestal.

D: There's a trace of face.

A: I make a note.

She takes out pad, takes pencil, makes to note.

D: Down the head. *(A at a loss. Irritably.)* Get going. Down his head. *(A puts back pad and pencil, goes to P, bows his head further, steps back.)* A shade more. *(A advances, bows the head further.)* Stop! *(A steps back.)* Fine. It's coming. *(Pause.)* Could do with more nudity.

A: I make a note.

She takes out pad, makes to take pencil.

D: Get going! Get going! *(A puts back the pad, goes to P, stands irresolute.)* Bare the neck. *(A undoes top buttons, parts the flaps, steps back.)* The legs. The shins. *(A advances, rolls up to below knee one trouser-leg, steps back.)* The other. *(Same for other leg, steps back.)* Higher. The knees. *(A advances, rolls up to above knees both trouser-legs, steps back.)* And whiten.

A: I make a note. *(She takes out pad, takes pencil, notes.)* Whiten all flesh.

D: It's coming. Is Luke around?

A: *(Calling.)* Luke! *(Pause. Louder.)* Luke!

L: *(Off, distant).* I hear you. *(Pause. Nearer.)* What's the trouble now?

A: Luke's around.

D: Blackout stage.

L: What?

A *transmits in technical terms. Fade-out of general light. Light on* **P** *alone.* **A** *in shadow.*

D: Just the head.

L: What?

A *transmits in technical terms. Fade-out of light on **P**'s body. Light on head alone. Long pause.*

D: Lovely. *Pause.*

A: *(Timidly).* What if he were to . . . were to . . . raise his head . . . an instant . . . show his face . . . just an instant.

D: For God's sake! What next? Raise his head! Where do you think we are? In Patagonia? Raise his head! For God's sake! *(Pause)* Good. There's our catastrophe. In the bag. Once more and I'm off.

A: *(to **L**.)* Once more and he's off.
*Fade-up of light on **P**'s body. Pause. Fade up of general light.*

D: Stop! *(Pause.)* Now . . . let 'em have it. *(Fade-out of general light. Pause. Fade-out of light on body. Light on head alone. Long pause.)*

Terrific! He'll have them on their feet. I can
hear it from here.

Pause. Distant storm of applause. **P** *raises his
head, fixes the audience. The applause falters,
dies.*

Long pause.

Fade-out of light on face.

What Where

What Where was first produced by Lucille Lortel and
The Harold Clurman Theatre, New York, New York,
on June 15, 1983. It was directed by Alan Schneider.

Bam	Donald Davis
Bom	David Warrilow
Bim	Rand Mitchell
Bem	Daniel Wirth
Voice of Bam	Donald Davis

Bam

Bem

Bim

Bom

Voice of Bam (V)

Note.

Players as alike as possible.

Same long grey gown.

Same long grey hair.

V in the shape of a small megaphone at head level.

Playing area (P) rectangle 3m x 2m, dimly lit, surrounded by shadow, stage right as seen from house. Downstage left, dimly lit, surrounded by shadow, V.

General dark.

Light on V.

Pause.

V: We are the last five.

In the present as were we still.

It is spring.

Time passes.

First without words.

I switch on.

Light on P.

Bam *at 3 head haught,* **Bom** *at 1 head bowed.*
Pause.

Not good.

I switch off.

Light off P.

I start again.

We are the last five.

It is spring.

Time passes.

First without words.

I switch on.

Light on P.
Bam *alone at 3 head haught.*
Pause.

Good.
I am alone.
It is spring.
Time passes.
First without words.
In the end Bom appears.
Reappears.

Bom *enters at N, halts at 1 head bowed.*
Pause.
Bim *enters at E, halts at 2 head haught.*

Pause.
Bim *exits at E followed by* **Bom**.
Pause.
Bim *enters at E, halts at 2 head bowed.*
Pause.
Bem *enters at N, halts at 1 head haught.*
Pause.

Bem *exits at N followed by* **Bim**.
Pause.
Bem *enters at N, halts at 1 head bowed.*
Pause.
Bam *exits at W followed by* **Bem**.
Pause.
Bam *enters at W, halts at 3 head bowed.*
Pause.

Good.
I switch off.

Light off P.

I start again.
We are the last five.
It is spring.
Time passes.
I switch on.

Light on P.
Bam *alone at 3 head haught.*
Pause.

Good.

I am alone.

It is spring.

Time passes.

Now with words.

In the end Bom appears.

Reappears.

Bom *enters at N, halts at l head bowed.*

Bam: Well?

Bom: *(Head bowed throughout).* Nothing.

Bam: He didn't say anything?

Bom: No

Bam: You gave him the works?

Bom: Yes.

Bam: And he didn't say anything?

Bom: No.

Bam: He wept?

Bom: Yes.

Bam: Screamed?

Bom: Yes.

Bam: Begged for mercy?

Bom: Yes.

Bam: But didn't say anything?

Bom: No.

V: Not good.
I start again.

Bam: Well?

Bom: Nothing.

Bam: He didn't say it?

V: Good.

Bom: No.

Bam: You gave him the works?

Bom: Yes.

Bam: And he didn't say it?

Bom: No.

Bam: He wept?

Bom: Yes.

Bam: Screamed?

Bom: Yes.

Bam: Begged for mercy?

Bom: Yes.

Bam: But didn't say it?

Bom: No.

Bam: Then why stop?

Bom: He passed out.

Bam: And you didn't revive him?

Bom: I tried.

Bam: Well?

Bom: I couldn't.

Pause.

Bam: It's a lie. *(Pause.)* He said it to you. *(Pause.)* Confess he said it to you. *(Pause.)* You'll be given the works until you confess.

V: Good.
In the end Bim appears.

Bim *enters at E, halts at 2 head haught.*

Bam: *(to* **Bim***).* Are you free?

Bim: Yes.

Bam: Take him away and give him the works until he confesses.

Bim: What must he confess?

Bam: That he said it to him.

Bim: Is that all?

Bam: Yes.

V: Not good.

I start again.

Bam: Take him away and give him the works until he confesses.

Bim: What must he confess?

Bam: That he said it to him.

Bim: Is that all?

Bam: And what.

V: Good.

Bim: Is that all?

Bam: Yes.

Bim: Then stop?

Bam: Yes.

Bim: Good. *(To* **Bom.***)* Come.

Bim *exits at E followed by* **Bom**.

V: Good.
I am alone.
It is summer.
Time passes.
In the end Bim appears.
Reappears.

Bim *enters at E, halts at 2 head bowed.*

Bam: Well?

Bim: *(Head bowed throughout).* Nothing.

Bam: He didn't say it?

Bim: No.

Bam: You gave him the works?

Bim: Yes.

Bam: And he didn't say it?

Bim: No.

V: Not good.
I start again.

Bam: Well?

Bim: Nothing.

Bam: He didn't say where?

V: Good.

Bim: Where?

V: Ah!

Bam: Where.

Bim: No.

Bam: You gave him the works?

Bim: Yes.

Bam: And he didn't say where?

Bim: No.

Bam: He wept?

Bim: Yes.

Bam: Screamed?

Bim: Yes.

Bam: Begged for mercy?

Bim: Yes.

Bam: But didn't say where?

Bim: No.

Bam: Then why stop?

Bim: He passed out.

Bam: And you didn't revive him?

Bim: I tried.

Bam: Well?

Bim: I couldn't.

Pause.

Bam: It's a lie. *(Pause.)* He said where to you. *(Pause.)* Confess he said where to you. *(Pause.)* You'll be given the works until you confess.

V: Good.
In the end Bem appears.

Bem *enters at N, halts at l head haught.*

Bam: *(to Bem).* Are you free?

Bem: Yes.

Bam: Take him away and give him the works until he confesses.

Bem: What must he confess?

Bam: That he said where to him.

Bem: Is that all?

Bam: Yes.

V: Not good.
I start again.

Bam: Take him away and give him the works until he confesses.

Bem: What must he confess?

Bam: That he said where to him.

Bem: Is that all?

Bam: And where.

V: Good.

Bem: Is that all?

Bam: Yes.

Bem: Then stop?

Bam: Yes.

Bem: Good. *(To* **Bim**.*)* Come.

Bem *exits at N followed by* **Bim**.

V: Good.

I am alone.

It is autumn.

Time passes.

In the end Bem appears.

Reappears.

Bem *enters at N, halts at 1 head bowed.*

Bam: Well?

Bem: *(Head bowed throughout).* Nothing.

Bam: He didn't say where?

Bem: No.

V: So on.

Bam: It's a lie. *(Pause.)* He said where to you.
(Pause.) Confess he said where to you. *(Pause.)*
You'll be given the works until you confess.

Bem: What must I confess?

Bam: That he said where to you.

Bem: Is that all?

Bam: And where.

Bem: Is that all?

Bam: Yes.

Bem: Then stop?

Bam: Yes. Come.

Bam *exits at W followed by* **Bem**.

V: Good.
It is winter.
Time passes.
In the end I appear.
Reappear.

Bam *enters at N, halts at 3 head bowed.*

V: Good.

I am alone.

In the present as were I still.

It is winter.

Without journey.

Time passes.

That is all.

Make sense who may.

I switch off.

Light off P.
Pause.
Light off V.

OTHER GROVE PRESS DRAMA AND THEATER PAPERBACKS

17061-X ARDEN, JOHN / Plays: One (Serjeant Musgrave's Dance, The Workhouse Donkey, Armstrong's Last Goodnight) / $4.95

17083-0 AYCKBOURN, ALAN / Absurd Person Singular, Absent Friends, Bedroom Farce: Three Plays / $3.95

17208-6 BECKETT, SAMUEL / Endgame / $4.95

17233-7 BECKETT, SAMUEL / Happy Days / $2.95

62061-5 BECKETT, SAMUEL / Ohio Impromptu, Catastrophe, What, Where: Three Plays / $4.95

17204-3 BECKETT, SAMUEL / Waiting for Godot / $3.50

17112-8 BRECHT, BERTOLT / Galileo / $2.95

17472-0 BRECHT, BERTOLT / The Threepenny Opera / $2.45

17411-9 CLURMAN, HAROLD / Nine Plays of the Modern Theater (Waiting for Godot by Samuel Beckett, The Visit by Friedrich Durrenmatt, Tango by Slawomir Mrozek, The Caucasian Chalk Circle by Bertolt Brecht, The Balcony by Jean Genet, Rhinoceros by Eugene Ionesco, American Buffalo by David Mamet, The Birthday Party by Harold Pinter, and Rosencrantz and Guildenstern Are Dead by Tom Stoppard) / $11.95

17535-2 COWARD, NOEL / Three Plays (Private Lives, Hay Fever, Blithe Spirit) / $4.50

17239-6 DURRENMATT, FRIEDRICH / The Visit / $4.95

17214-0 GENET, JEAN / The Balcony / $5.95

17390-2 GENET, JEAN / The Maids and Deathwatch: Two Plays/ $5.95

17075-X INGE, WILLIAM / Four Plays (Come Back, Little Sheba; Picnic; Bus Stop; The Dark at the Top of the Stairs) / $7.95

17267-1 IONESCO, EUGENE / Exit the King / $2.95

17209-4 IONESCO, EUGENE / Four Plays (The Bald Soprano, The Lesson, The Chairs, Jack or The Submission) / $4.95

17226-4 IONESCO, EUGENE / Rhinoceros and Other Plays (The Leader, The Future Is in Eggs, or It Takes All Sorts to Make a World) / $4.95

17485-2 JARRY, ALFRED / The Ubu Plays (Ubu Rex, Ubu Cuckolded, Ubu Enchained) / $9.95

17744-4 KAUFMAN, GEORGE and HART, MOSS / Three Plays (Once in A Lifetime; You Can't Take It With You; The Man Who Came to Dinner) / $6.95

17016-4 MAMET, DAVID / American Buffalo / $4.95
17040-7 MAMET, DAVID / A Life in the Theatre / $6.95
17043-1 MAMET, DAVID / Sexual Perversity in Chicago and The Duck Variations / $5.95
17264-7 MROZEK, SLAWOMIR / Tango / $3.95
17092-X ODETS, CLIFFORD / Six Plays (Waiting for Lefty; Awake and Sing; Golden Boy; Rocket to the Moon; Till the Day I Die; Paradise Lost) / $7.95
17001-6 ORTON, JOE / The Complete Plays (The Ruffian on the Stair, The Good and Faithful Servant, The Erpingham Camp, Funeral Games, Loot, What the Butler Saw, Entertaining Mr. Sloane) / $6.95
17019-9 PINTER, HAROLD / Complete Works: One (The Birthday Party, The Room, The Dumb Waiter, A Slight Ache, A Night Out, The Black and White, The Examination) / $6.95
17020-2 PINTER, HAROLD / Complete Works: Two (The Caretaker, Night School, The Dwarfs, The Collection, The Lover, Five Revue Sketches) / $6.95
17251-5 PINTER, HAROLD / The Homecoming / $4.95
17885-8 PINTER, HAROLD / No Man's Land / $3.95
17539-5 POMERANCE, BERNARD / The Elephant Man / $4.25
17743-6 RATTIGAN, TERENCE / Plays: One /.$5.95
17948-X SHAWN, WALLACE and GREGORY, ANDRE / My Dinner with André / $5.95
17884-X STOPPARD, TOM / Travesties / $3.95
17260-4 STOPPARD, TOM / Rosencrantz and Guildenstern Are Dead / $3.95
17206-X WALEY, ARTHUR, tr. and ed. / The No Plays of Japan / $7.95

GROVE PRESS, 841 Broadway, New York, N.Y. 10003